Editor
Eric Migliaccio

Editor in Chief
Karen J. Goldfluss, M.S. Ed.

Creative Director
Sarah M. Smith

Cover Artist
Barb Lorseyedi

Art Coordinator
Renée Mc Elwee

Illustrator
Clint McKnight

Imaging
James Edward Grace

Publisher
Mary D. Smith, M.S. Ed.

Author
Heather Wolpert-

For correlations to Common Core State Standards, see page 8 of this book or visit *http://www.teachercreated.com/standards/.*

Teacher Created Resources
6421 Industry Way
Westminster, CA 92683
www.teachercreated.com

ISBN: 978-1-4206-3827-1

Made in U.S.A.

Table of Contents

Introduction

Reading and comprehending nonfiction or informational text is a challenge. Not everyone can do it well, and it needs to be specifically taught. Students who are great at reading narratives like *Lord of the Rings* or *The Princess Diaries* may still quiver at the possibility of having to understand instructions on uploading an assignment to DropBox. Students who love reading historical fiction may be fearful of reading history. Students who, with flashlight in hand, hide beneath their sheets reading the end of a science-fiction book may glaze over at the sight of an actual factual science article.

Nevertheless, informational text is all around us, and reading it well just takes working out a certain muscle — an informational-text muscle, if you will.

This book is meant to be an informational-muscle gym. Each activity is meant to build in complexity, and each activity is meant to push students in both their reading and their ability to display what they understand about what they read.

In addition to a practice passage, there are 18 reading selections contained in this book. The selections are separated into units, based on their subject matter. As a result, no matter the content area you teach, you will find applicable selections here on which your students can practice.

It doesn't matter what state you teach in, what grade level you teach, or what subject you teach; this book will aid students in understanding more deeply the difficult task of reading informational and nonfiction texts.

Reading Comprehension and the Common Core

The Common Core Standards are here, and with them come a different way to think about reading comprehension. In the past, reading informational text had been compartmentalized, each piece an isolated activity. The Common Core way of thinking is slightly different.

The goal is for students to read different genres and selections of text, pull them together in their heads, and be able to derive a theme or topic that may be shared by them all. In other words, a student may be given three different texts from three different points of view or three different genre standpoints and then have to think about their own thoughts on the subject.

Perhaps a student looks at the following:

1. Instructions on downloading an image from a digital camera
2. A biography about a famous photographer
3. A Google search history on the invention of the camera from the past to the present

Then, from those pieces, the student must pull a common theme or opinion on the topic.

Introduction *(cont.)*

Reading Comprehension and the Common Core *(cont.)*

But to be able to synthesize text (put the thoughts together), a student must first be able to read individual texts and analyze them (pull them apart). That's where this series of books comes in.

Nonfiction Reading Comprehension for the Common Core helps students to hone in on a specific piece of text, identify what's the most important concept in that piece, and answer questions about that specific selection. This will train your students for the bigger challenge that will come later in their schooling: viewing multiple texts and shaking out the meaning of them all.

If you are a public-school teacher, you may be in a state that has adopted the Common Core Standards. Use the selections in this book as individual reading-comprehension activities or pair them with similarly themed selections from other genres to give students a sense of how they will have to pull understanding from the informational, text-heavy world around us.

Copy the individual worksheets as is; or, if you are looking for a more Common Core-aligned format, mimic the Common Core multiple-choice assessments that are coming our way by entering the questions into websites that can help create computer adaptive tests (CATs).

CATs are assessments that allow a student to answer a question, which, depending on whether they answered it correctly or not, leads them to the next question that may be more geared to his or her level. In other words, each student will be taking a differentiated assessment that will end up indicating if a student is capable of answering "Novice" questions up to "Expert" questions.

There are many websites out there that can help you develop assessments to mimic those planned. Create the quiz and embed it into your class webpage or document:

Here are just a couple:

- *http://www.gotoquiz.com/create.html*
- *http://www.quibblo.com/*

Use the selections from this book, and then enter the corresponding questions into the quiz generators. We have identified questions that are higher or lower in level by assigning them a "weight" (from single-weight up through triple-weight). This weight system provides a glimpse of how hard a student should work in order to answer the question correctly. (For more information, read "Leveled Questions" on page 5.)

Regardless of how you choose to use this book, introducing students to the informational world at large is an important way to help them build skills that they will use throughout their schooling and beyond.

Introduction *(cont.)*

Leveled Questions

As you go through this book, you will notice that each question that students will be answering is labeled with icons that look like weights. These icons represent different levels of difficulty. The levels are based on Costa's Levels of Questioning.

The questions in this book are divided into three levels:

Level 1

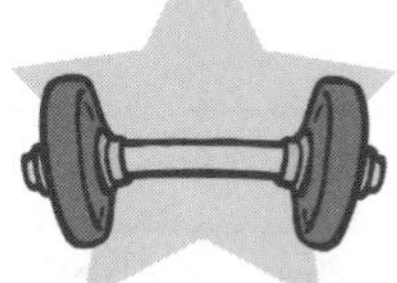

These include sentence stems that ask students to . . .

Recite
Define
Describe
List

Level 2

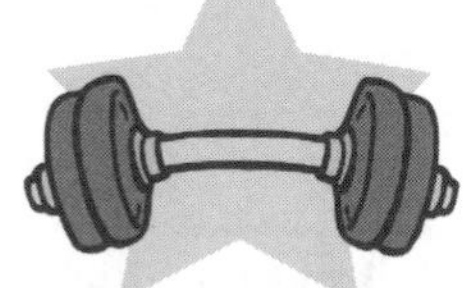

These include sentence stems that ask students to . . .

Infer
Compare/Contrast
Sequence
Categorize

Level 3

These include sentence stems that ask students to . . .

Judge
Evaluate
Create
Hypothesize
Predict

The icons are a visual way to make these levels clear to students. That is important because students need to be able to recognize that some questions may require more effort and thought to answer.

Now, most of the multiple-choice questions in this book happen to fall into the Level 1 and Level 2 categories. That is pretty standard for multiple-choice questions. After all, how can asking to create something be defined by an A, B, C, or D answer? However, we may have found a way around that.

At the end of each worksheet is a place for students to develop their own questions about the material they have just read. This brings in a deeper-thinking opportunity. Having your students ask higher-level questions is a great way for assessing their comprehension of what they have read. The deeper the student's question, the deeper his or her understanding of the material.

A student handout called "The Questioning Rubric" is provided on page 6. It serves two purposes:

- It gives your students concrete examples of the elements that make up the different levels of questions.
- It gives you, the teacher, a way to determine whether a student-generated question is a low- or high-level inquiry.

The goal of a student is to ask more challenging questions of oneself. The goal of the teacher is to be able to track better the level of production for each student. This book helps do both.

Introduction *(cont.)*

The Questioning Rubric

Answering questions is one way of proving you understand a reading selection. However, creating your very own questions about the selection might be an even better way. Developing thoughtful, high-level questions can really display your understanding of what you have read, and it also makes other students think about the reading passage in a unique way.

So what types of questions can you ask? There are three levels of questions, and for each one there is a different amount of work your brain must do to answer the question. We've chosen to use a symbol of a weight in order to represent this amount. Consult this chart when thinking about what defines a great question as compared to a so-so one.

Icon	Description
	A single weight represents a **Level 1** question that doesn't require much brainpower to answer correctly. The question only asks readers to tell what they know about the selection. For example, any inquiry that asks for a simple "Yes or No" or "True or False" response is a Level 1 question.
	A double weight represents a **Level 2** question that requires you to use a little more brain sweat. (Ewww!) This question asks readers to think a little beyond the passage. It may require some analysis, inference, or interpretation. Questions involving comparing/contrasting or sequencing often fall here.
	A **Level 3** question really makes you work for its answer. These questions allow you to show off your knowledge of a topic by asking you to create, wonder, judge, evaluate, and/or apply what you know to what you think. These types of questions are much more open-ended than Level 1 or Level 2 questions.

Don't be scared to sweat a little in answering or developing Level 3 questions. Working out your brain in this way will help prepare you for some heavy lifting later on in life. So as you progress through this book, use this rubric as a resource to make sure your questions are as high-level as possible.

Need help getting started? The following sentence stems will give you ideas about how to create questions for each level.

Level 1

- Write the definition of...
- Describe how _____ is...
- List the details that go into...

Level 2

- What can you infer from _____?
- Compare _____ with _____.
- Contrast _____ with _____.
- Write the steps in sequence from _____.
- Place _____ in the right category.

Level 3

- How would you judge the _____?
- How would you evaluate the _____?
- How can you create a _____?
- Hypothesize what would happen if _____.
- What do you predict will happen in _____?

Introduction *(cont.)*

Achievement Graph

As you correct your responses in this book, track how well you improve. Calculate how many answers you got right after each worksheet and mark your progress here based on the number of weights each question was worth. For instance, if you get the first problem correct, and it is worth two weights, then write "2" in the first column. Do this for each column, and add up your total at the end.

Reading Passage	1	2	3	4	Total
"A Storytelling Tradition"					
"Pluto: Planet or No?"					
"My Foot Fell Asleep"					
"More Than a Long Neck"					
"Light Before Sound"					
"How to Debug a Computer"					
"A Female Pharaoh?"					
"The Library of Alexandria"					
"Finding the Rosetta Stone"					
"One Massive Mystery"					
"The Story Behind the Beard"					
"The Man Who Made Myths Cool"					
"A Teacher for All Times"					
"Her Words Live On"					
"Bo Knows Greatness"					
"What Is Microlending?"					
"Mastering an Ancient Art"					
"From Postcards to Pizza"					
"A Dangerous Delicacy"					

Common Core State Standards

The lessons and activities included in *Nonfiction Reading Comprehension for the Common Core, Grade 6* meet the following Common Core State Standards. (©Copyright 2010. National Governors Association Center for Best Practices and Council of Chief State School Officers. All right reserved.) For more information about the Common Core State Standards, go to *http://www.corestandards.org/* or visit *http://www.teachercreated.com/standards/*.

Informational Text Standards	
Key Ideas and Details	**Pages**
CCSS.ELA.RI.6.1. Cite textual evidence to support analysis of what the text says explicitly as well as inferences drawn from the text.	10–47
Craft and Structure	**Pages**
CCSS.ELA.RI.6.4. Determine the meaning of words and phrases as they are used in a text, including figurative, connotative, and technical meanings.	10–47
Range of Reading and Level of Text Complexity	**Pages**
CCSS.ELA.RI.6.10. By the end of the year, read and comprehend informational texts, including history/social studies, science, and technical texts, at the high end of the grades 6–8 text complexity band proficiently.	10–47
Language Standards	
Conventions of Standard English	**Pages**
CCSS.ELA.L.6.1. Demonstrate command of the conventions of standard English grammar and usage when writing or speaking.	11–47
CCSS.ELA.L.6.2. Demonstrate command of the conventions of standard English capitalization, punctuation, and spelling when writing.	11–47
Knowledge of Language	**Pages**
CCSS.ELA.L.6.3. Use knowledge of language and its conventions when writing, speaking, reading, or listening.	10–47
Vocabulary Acquisition and Use	**Pages**
CCSS.ELA.L.6.4. Determine or clarify the meaning of unknown and multiple-meaning words and phrases based on *grade 6 reading and content*, choosing flexibly from a range of strategies.	10–47
CCSS.ELA.L.6.5. Demonstrate understanding of figurative language, word relationships, and nuances in word meanings.	10–47
CCSS.ELA.L.6.6. Acquire and use accurately grade-appropriate general academic and domain-specific words and phrases; gather vocabulary knowledge when considering a word or phrase important to comprehension or expression.	10–47
Language Standards	
Research to Build and Present Knowledge	**Pages**
CCSS.ELA.W.6.9. Draw evidence from literary or informational texts to support analysis, reflection, and research.	10–47

Multiple-Choice Test-Taking Tips

Some multiple-choice questions are straightforward and easy. "I know the answer!" your brain yells right away. Some questions, however, stump even the most prepared student. In cases like that, you have to make an educated guess. An educated guess is a guess that uses what you know to help guide your attempt. You don't put your hand over your eyes and pick a random letter! You select it because you've thought about the format of the question, the word choice, the other possible answers, and the language of what's being asked. By making an educated guess, you're increasing your chances of guessing correctly. Whenever you are taking a multiple-choice assessment, you should remember to follow the rules below:

1. Read the directions. It's crucial. You may assume you know what is being asked, but sometimes directions can be tricky when you least expect them to be.
2. Read the questions before you read the passage. Doing this allows you to read the text through a more educated and focused lens. For example, if you know that you will be asked to identify the main idea, you can be on the lookout for that ahead of time.
3. Don't skip a question. Instead, try to make an educated guess. That starts with crossing off the ones you definitely know are not the correct answer. For instance, if you have four possible answers (A, B, C, D) and you can cross off two of them immediately, you've doubled your chances of guessing correctly. If you don't cross off any obvious ones, you would only have a 25% chance of guessing right. However, if you cross off two, you now have a 50% chance!
4. Read carefully for words like *always*, *never*, *not*, *except*, and *every*. Words like these are there to make you stumble. They make the question very specific. Sometimes an answer can be right some of the time, but if a word like *always* or *every* is in the question, the answer must be right *all of the time.*
5. After reading a question, try to come up with the answer first in your head before looking at the possible answers. That way, you will be less likely to bubble or click something you aren't sure about.
6. In questions with an "All of the Above" answer, think of it this way: if you can identify at least two that are correct, then "All of the Above" is probably the correct answer.
7. In questions with a "None of the Above" answer, think of it this way: if you can identify at least two that are *not* correct, then "None of the Above" is probably the correct answer.
8. Don't keep changing your answer. Unless you are sure you made a mistake, usually the first answer you chose is the right one.

Practice Passage

A Storytelling Tradition

North America is full of folklore. A culture's folklore includes the stories that its people tell that teach about their traditions. The stories include the beliefs of the people, and they are usually passed down by word of mouth. That is, the older people tell the younger people. When the young people grow up, they tell their children the same stories. Every culture has its own folklore.

Native-American stories have lived through the tradition of folklore. The stories were created to help explain what happened in the world around the Native Americans. Some stories explained what happened in nature. Others explained how Earth was created. For instance, one Cherokee myth tells the story of how Earth was once a floating island. It hung on cords, and the sun was on a track that moved from east to west. This story was an explanation of a natural phenomenon.

Some stories were tales of heroes. Others were tales of "tricksters." Tricksters are characters who taught the listener how not to behave. Many of the stories included lessons. These lessons warned the people about how to behave. The lessons are called morals.

Native-American tribes passed down their folklore from father to son and mother to daughter. This way, everyone would remember the lessons from year to year. This was how the stories lived from year to year, decade to decade, and century to century.

Answer the following questions about the story "A Storytelling Tradition." The weights show you how hard you will need to work to find each answer.

1. According to the passage, folklore was passed down through "word of mouth." What can you infer is the meaning of this phrase?

Ⓐ People passed down stories using written words.
Ⓑ People passed down stories by sharing audio files.
Ⓒ People passed down stories by telling those stories to others.
Ⓓ People passed down stories by sharing books.

2. What tribe told the story of the floating island?

Ⓐ North America
Ⓑ the Apache
Ⓒ the Cherokee
Ⓓ the Mayans

3. According to the passage, what is the opposite of a hero?

Ⓐ a son
Ⓑ a trickster
Ⓒ a daughter
Ⓓ a warning

4. According to the Cherokee myth from the passage, the sun "moved on a track from east to west." What is the story trying to explain?

Ⓐ why we have the tides
Ⓑ why we have earthquakes
Ⓒ the creation of the animals
Ⓓ why the sun rises in the east and sets in the west

On the lines below, write your own question based on "A Storytelling Tradition." Circle the correct picture on the left to show the level of the question you wrote.

____

____

____

____

____

On a separate piece of paper . . .

- Write a sentence that includes the word *folklore*.
- What stories do you know that come from your culture?

Science Passage #1

Pluto: Planet or Not?

Have you heard the story of the former planet Pluto? In 1915, scientists thought they saw hints of a new planet way out in deep space. Then, in 1930, it was announced that a little planet had been discovered. It was made of rock and ice, and it was about $\frac{1}{6}$ the size of the Earth's moon. It became known as the 9th planet in our solar system.

The name for this 9th planet was suggested by an 11-year-old English girl named Venetia Burney. In mythology, Pluto was the name of the ruler of the underworld. Venetia thought that "Pluto" would then be an appropriate name for such a cold, dark planet. This name was put to a vote, along with two others: Minerva and Cronus. On March 24, 1930, "Pluto" was unanimously chosen for the name of the new planet.

Unfortunately for Pluto, being called the 9th planet would not last. Scientists changed the definition of the word *planet*, and little Pluto no longer fit into the new definition. They said that in order for an object to be a planet, it must satisfy these criteria:

1. It must be massive enough to hold the shape of a sphere.
2. It's gravitational pull must be so strong that it clears out other objects in its area.
3. It must be in orbit around the Sun.

Pluto did not fit the second rule. Besides, there were bigger bodies in space that were not called planets. So in 2006, scientists downgraded Pluto from a "planet" to a "dwarf planet." Pluto lost its status, but at least it got to keep its well-loved name!

Name: ______________________________ Science Passage #1

Answer the following questions about the story "Pluto: Planet or Not?" The weights show you how hard you will need to work to find each answer.

1. Based on the passage, what does the phrase "clears out" mean?

Ⓐ destroys
Ⓑ moves away
Ⓒ lights up
Ⓓ races by

2. Based on the passage, what do you think the author's attitude is about Pluto?

Ⓐ The author hates the planet.
Ⓑ The author feels sympathy for the planet.
Ⓒ The author disagrees with the decision.
Ⓓ The author likes mythology.

3. Which is not given in the passage as a way that scientists define a planet?

Ⓐ It has to orbit around the Sun.
Ⓑ It has to have a certain amount of gravity.
Ⓒ It has to have rings.
Ⓓ It has to have a spherical shape.

4. How long was Pluto known as an official planet?

Ⓐ about 17 years
Ⓑ about 6 years
Ⓒ about 76 years
Ⓓ about 30 years

On the lines below, write your own question based on "Pluto: Planet or Not?" Circle the correct picture on the left to show the level of the question you wrote.

____

____

____

____

____

On a separate piece of paper . . .

- Write a sentence that includes the word *downgraded*.
- What would you name a planet? Why would you name it that?

Science Passage #2

My Foot Fell Asleep!

It's a strange sensation. It's an odd feeling. Something seems to be wrong with your foot. It tingles, and it just won't move as naturally it normally does. With every step, tiny pins seem to be pricking just below the surface of your skin. You wonder, "What's happening, and when will I be able to walk normally again?"

Has this ever happened to you? You've probably felt something similar to this after sitting for a long period of time with your foot tucked under your body. When you tried to straighten out your leg, that's when you noticed the odd tingling. Many of us have a way to describe this unsettling sensation. We say, "My foot fell asleep!"

It all starts with the nerves you have winding throughout your body. Nerves are like thin threads or wires that constantly carry messages back and forth between your brain and your body. Functioning like incredibly high-speed telephone wires, these nerves help you communicate with yourself. For example, let's say your shoulder brushes up against a scalding-hot surface. Nerves in your shoulder send your brain a message that basically says, "Hot! Remove shoulder now!" In a flash, you remove your shoulder from the source of the heat. This communication happens instantaneously. It happens so quickly that you are not even aware of having received the message.

So how does this explain the sensation of your foot falling asleep? Well, you usually feel that sensation after you've been sitting on your foot for a long time. This activity puts too much weight on the nerves in your foot and lower leg. It squishes them down, and this cuts off the connection between the nerves and your brain. Luckily, the solution to this problem is simple: just stop pressing down on those nerves and start moving your foot around. At first, your foot will tingle, and it won't move the way in which you are accustomed. Fortunately, you are not injured in any way and so that feeling won't last for very long. It just takes a few moments for the connection to restore itself. Before long, the connection comes back completely. It's as if your foot has woken up!

Answer the following questions about the story "My Foot Fell Asleep!" The weights show you how hard you will need to work to find each answer.

1. To what does the author of this piece compare the nerves in your body?

Ⓐ scalding-hot surfaces
Ⓑ high-speed computers
Ⓒ high-speed telephone wires
Ⓓ flashing sirens

2. After reading the passage, what can you infer is happening in your body (and everyone else's) right now?

Ⓐ Your nerves are sending messages to your brain.
Ⓑ Your foot is falling asleep.
Ⓒ You're feeling an odd tingling sensation.
Ⓓ Your foot is not moving normally.

3. Which of these words has a very different meaning than the others?

Ⓐ oddly
Ⓑ strangely
Ⓒ unnaturally
Ⓓ instantaneously

4. If you were to put these four things in the order in which they happen, which would happen third?

Ⓐ Your brain sends a signal to your hand to remove it.
Ⓑ Your hand touches a hot pan.
Ⓒ You remove your hand from the hot pan.
Ⓓ Your nerves send a signal to your brain, saying "Hot pan!"

On the lines below, write your own question based on "My Foot Fell Asleep!" Circle the correct picture on the left to show the level of the question you wrote.

____

____

____

____

____

On a separate piece of paper . . .

- Write a sentence that includes the word *connection.*
- Can you remember a time when your foot fell asleep? Describe how it felt.

Science Passage #3

More Than a Long Neck

What would your answer be if you were asked, "What makes a giraffe so tall?" Would you immediately say "its neck"? This would be an understandable reply, since a giraffe's neck can grow to over six feet in length! It is a unique and vital tool that a giraffe uses to survive in the wild. For example, giraffes need their elongated necks to feed on the leaves of tall trees and to balance themselves as they run. They even use their necks as weapons when they fight. But the neck isn't the only physical feature that makes giraffes so unusually tall: they also have extremely long legs.

Just like its neck, a giraffe's legs are very useful and vital. Their long legs give them that extra height they need to reach those tall trees. And even though a giraffe's legs look very thin, they are incredibly powerful. Giraffes use them to run at speeds of up to 37 miles per hour. They also use their legs for protection. A mother giraffe, for example, will kick at animals that are attacking her babies.

Having long legs does not always make things easy on giraffes, however. First of all, giraffes need to drink water, so they must get their mouths down to the ground where the water is. Their long legs can make this maneuver very difficult. When a giraffe wants to reach down to drink water, it basically has two options: it can spread its front legs wide open, or it can bend its knees. A giraffe cannot drop its head down to the ground without doing one of those two things.

Also, giraffes have needed to adapt the way they walk. Most four-legged animals walk by moving their left front leg and right back leg forward at the same time. The next step moves their right front leg and left back leg forward. This is sometimes referred to as the "diagonal walk." Giraffes have such long legs, however, that they cannot do this. Their front legs would crash into their back legs, and they would trip themselves. Instead, they have to move the legs on one side of their body at the same time. A giraffe walks by swinging both legs on one side forward and then swinging both legs on the other side forward.

Answer the following questions about the story "More Than a Long Neck." The weights show you how hard you will need to work to find each answer.

1. According to the passage, what is an advantage of having a long neck?

Ⓐ eating birds from tall trees
Ⓑ seeing over tall hills
Ⓒ drinking water from rivers
Ⓓ eating leaves from tall trees

2. What can't a giraffe do?

Ⓐ bend its knees
Ⓑ run over 35 miles per hour
Ⓒ do a "diagonal walk"
Ⓓ use its neck to fight

3. What is another word for *vital*?

Ⓐ elongated
Ⓑ needed
Ⓒ adapted
Ⓓ physical

4. Which of these describes how a giraffe walks?

Ⓐ left front leg and left back leg together, then right front leg and right back leg together
Ⓑ left front leg and right back leg together, then right front leg and left back leg together
Ⓒ both front legs together, then both back legs together
Ⓓ all four legs move forward at the same time

On the lines below, write your own question based on "More Than a Long Neck." Circle the correct picture on the left to show the level of the question you wrote.

____

____

____

____

____

On a separate piece of paper . . .

- Write a sentence that includes the word *adapt*.
- What is the most surprising fact you read in this passage about giraffes? Explain your choice.

Science Passage #4

Light Before Sound

Imagine you are lying in your bedroom on a dark, stormy night. Rain is pelting your bedroom window, and you can hear the wind whipping through the branches of your neighbor's enormous oak tree. Suddenly, a flash of bright light illuminates your room, as if a large lamp quickly switched on and then off. Seconds later, a noise seems to roll through your room. The sound grows louder, until a deafening crack nearly jolts you out of your bed. What just happened?

You have just experienced a natural event that we usually refer to as "thunder and lightning." Maybe, though, we should reverse the order and say "lightning and thunder." Think about it. What did you experience first, the thunder or the lightning? If you had been outside and looking up at the sky, you would have first seen a bolt of lightning light up the sky. Then, moments later, you would hear the loud boom of thunder. The lightning and the thunder don't seem to happen simultaneously.

But here's the truth: the lightning (light) and thunder (sound) *do* happen together and at the same time. So why do we see the lightning before we hear the thunder? The answer lies in the fact that light travels faster than sound. Light travels at about 186,000 miles per second! Sound "only" travels about 770 miles per hour. So the light gets to our eyes much more quickly than the sound gets to our ears.

Thunder and lightning are just one example of this phenomenon. You might have witnessed another example of this natural occurrence if you've ever attended a sporting event. Let's say you're at a baseball game, and you're sitting in the outfield bleachers, hundreds of feet from home plate. You see the pitcher deliver the pitch and the batter swing, but it takes a split second before you hear the crack of the wooden bat making contact with the ball. Once again, you experience it this way because light travels faster than sound.

Answer the following questions about the story "Light Before Sound." The weights show you how hard you will need to work to find each answer.

1. Based on the passage, which of these words is an antonym of *deafening*?

Ⓐ thunderous
Ⓑ hushed
Ⓒ noisy
Ⓓ loud

2. About how fast does sound travel?

Ⓐ 770 miles per second
Ⓑ 770 miles per hour
Ⓒ 186,000 miles per second
Ⓓ 186,000 miles per hour

3. Imagine you're at a baseball game. A batter hits a ball hard but right at a fielder, who catches the ball. Which of these events would you experience third?

Ⓐ hearing the batter hitting the ball
Ⓑ hearing the fielder catch a ball
Ⓒ seeing the batter swing at the ball
Ⓓ seeing the fielder catch a ball

4. Which of these words from the passage most closely means "falling quickly and heavily"?

Ⓐ contacting
Ⓑ deafening
Ⓒ whipping
Ⓓ pelting

On the lines below, write your own question based on "Light Before Sound." Circle the correct picture on the left to show the level of the question you wrote.

____

____

____

____

____

On a separate piece of paper . . .

- Write a sentence that includes the word *simultaneously*.
- Think of one more example when you might witness something from far away and see it happen before you hear it happen.

Science Passage #5

How to Debug a Computer

If an office worker's computer stalls or behaves strangely, that person might say, "My computer is acting buggy!" If enough people complained, an engineer back in the company might eventually say, "We need to debug this software." People use the word *bug* to describe a glitch in how a computer operates.

Usually, this means that there is a technical "bug" in the system. In fact, there is a record of Thomas Edison referring to such a thing all the way back in 1878. However, there was one time of which we know when the phrase was used to mean an actual bug!

Back in 1947, scientist and military woman Grace Hopper and her team were testing a "calculator" at Harvard University. This calculator was not what you might be picturing. It was not the type of device that could fit in the palm of your hand. No, computers were much different back then, and this one was a huge contraption, big enough to fill a room. Hopper's team was called in to determine why this enormous machine was not functioning properly. In doing this, they found that something was wrong with the relay system. The scientists who were working on it investigated. They looked further and tried harder to locate the problem. Do you know what they found? They discovered a dead moth that had gotten trapped within the device.

Once they found the moth, the operators pinned it to the computer log. In the log, they wrote, "First actual case of bug being found." They put out the word that they had "debugged" the machine, and this is how the phrase "debugging a computer program" was born. In 1988, the log, with the moth still taped onto the page, was on display in the Naval Surface Warfare Center Computer Museum in Virginia. It was moved to the Smithsonian Museum in 1991. The log, along with the moth carcass, can still be viewed there today.

Answer the following questions about the story "How to Debug a Computer." The weights show you how hard you will need to work to find each answer.

1. Based on the passage, what does the word *debugging* mean?

Ⓐ fixing
Ⓑ taping
Ⓒ trapping
Ⓓ discovering

2. What can you infer the word *device* is referring to at the end of the third paragraph?

Ⓐ the moth
Ⓑ the log
Ⓒ the computer
Ⓓ the museum

3. What kind of bug was found in the computer?

Ⓐ a bee
Ⓑ an ant
Ⓒ a moth
Ⓓ a cockroach

4. Based on what is said in the passage, you can predict that computers are getting

Ⓐ bigger.
Ⓑ more powerful.
Ⓒ more complex.
Ⓓ smaller.

On the lines below, write your own question based on "How to Debug a Computer." Circle the correct picture on the left to show the level of the question you wrote.

____

____

____

____

____

On a separate piece of paper . . .

- Write a sentence that includes the word *investigated.*
- Sometimes, things go wrong when we use computers. Describe a time when your computer wasn't doing what you needed it to do and how you solved the problem.

History Passage #1

A Female Pharaoh?

Ancient Egypt was not known for its female rulers. However, that doesn't mean that there weren't any. In fact, one of the most influential pharaohs was female. Her name was Hatshepsut, and she ruled from about 1479 BCE to 1458 BCE. This was way before the ancient Romans began their empire and way before the ancient Greeks created their myths. So just how did this young woman become in charge of an entire powerful nation?

Young Hatshepsut was 12 when her father, the king, died. She then married her stepbrother, and he became pharaoh. The tradition of marrying people from your own family was normal in ancient Egypt because they believed it kept the royal bloodlines pure. When her husband died, the heir to the throne became an infant boy named Thutmose III. Because this heir was so young, Hatshepsut made all of the decisions for him. After about a year of this arrangement, she declared herself pharaoh. To ensure that she was not questioned about her role, she started telling her people that she was chosen by the god Aman-Ra for the job. Then, she began having pictures of herself created with the traditional clothes of a pharaoh, including a false beard! However, what is really interesting is how unique she was as a ruler.

Hatshepsut's time as pharaoh was a time of great prosperity for Egypt. While many pharaohs focused on war, she focused on building and trade as a way to strengthen her nation. Under her rule, great buildings were constructed and riches were brought back from other lands.

She reigned for about 20 years, until she died of unknown causes. Thutmose III became pharoah at that point. Soon after, he attempted to wipe all traces of Hatshepsut from record. Many monuments built to Hapshepsut were destroyed. Walls were built around others. Why did he do this? Many believe it was so that no one would question that his son would be the next heir to the throne.

Name: ______________________________

Answer the following questions about the story "A Female Pharaoh?" The weights show you how hard you will need to work to find each answer.

1. Why were royal family members told to marry each other?

Ⓐ so that they could be stronger
Ⓑ so that they wouldn't have to change their name
Ⓒ so that that the bloodline remained pure
Ⓓ so that they knew everybody at all their events

2. According to the passage, why was Hatshepsut so unique?

Ⓐ She liked going to war.
Ⓑ She married her stepbrother.
Ⓒ She grew a beard.
Ⓓ She focused on building and trade.

3. Based on the passage, what can you infer is the meaning of *prosperity*?

Ⓐ wealth
Ⓑ war
Ⓒ family
Ⓓ tradition

4. According to the passage, what did Thutmose III try to do?

Ⓐ Rule Egypt when he was an infant.
Ⓑ Kill Hatshepsut so he could be pharaoh.
Ⓒ Erase all evidence that Hatshepsut had been pharaoh.
Ⓓ Go to war with Hatshepsut so he could win back the throne.

On the lines below, write your own question based on "A Female Pharaoh?" Circle the correct picture on the left to show the level of the question you wrote.

____

____

____

____

____

On a separate piece of paper . . .

- Write a sentence that includes the word *traditional*.
- Do you remember what it was like to be too young to do something you wanted to do? How did you feel seeing others do those things?

History Passage #2

The Library of Alexandria

Just imagine a library that has every book ever written. That was the goal of the rulers who built the Library of Alexandria in Egypt. This great building was imagined and built either during the reign of Ptolemy I or his son, Ptolemy II. It is not know for sure when it was constructed, but it is known that the Library played an important role in Egyptian culture during that era.

The library was huge. It had to be, since it was designed to be a collection of all the world's stories, philosophies, theories, and knowledge! Scholars believe it probably looked a lot like a college or university of today. They believe it included gardens, a dining area, meeting rooms, lecture halls, and lots of books and scrolls. In fact, the local port had a rule that any book on any ship coming into port had to be left for copying. The original would be returned to its owner only after the library had a duplicate. Egypt even sent out people to book fairs beyond its own lands. They found books in places like Athens and Rhodes, and they brought them back to the library. What *foresight* the Egyptians had! They realized how important it would be to have such a collection, and they put the steps in place to create the most unique library ever assembled.

Unfortunately, it was not to last. Historians believe that during the Roman Conquest, Julius Caesar set fire to the library. He may even have done this by accident. The building and all it contained was lost forever. Still, the legend that it left behind helps to fuel future dreams. In fact, a similar library is now being "built." Its goal is to collect all the books ever printed and provide them in one online library. It's a new Library of Alexandria for a new century.

Name: ______________________________

Answer the following questions about the story "The Library of Alexandria." The weights show you how hard you will need to work to find each answer.

1. What was the purpose of the Library of Alexandria?

Ⓐ to collect all the stories known to man
Ⓑ to learn about other cultures, philosophies, and theories
Ⓒ to gather as much knowledge as possible
Ⓓ All of the above.

2. Based on the passage, what can you infer is meant by "having foresight"?

Ⓐ thinking ahead
Ⓑ being excited
Ⓒ being unsure
Ⓓ thinking creatively

3. Who possibly destroyed the Library of Alexandria?

Ⓐ Cleopatra
Ⓑ Ptolemy I
Ⓒ Ptolemy II
Ⓓ Julius Caesar

4. Why don't we know for sure what the library looked like?

Ⓐ It was too big to see all of it.
Ⓑ It was burned down.
Ⓒ It was all moved online.
Ⓓ It was sold in book fairs.

On the lines below, write your own question based on "The Library of Alexandria." Circle the correct picture on the left to show the level of the question you wrote.

____

____

____

____

____

On a separate piece of paper . . .

- Write a sentence that includes the word *assembled.*
- Have you ever lost something that was priceless? Something that is priceless has so much value that no money in the world could buy it again. What happened, and how did you feel?

History Passage #3

Finding the Rosetta Stone

Long ago, artwork was discovered on Egyptian tombs. And for a long time, archeologists and scientists couldn't figure out what all these pictures meant. They couldn't understand the artifacts they found from the ancient Egyptian culture. The symbols on the walls, tombs, and vases clearly represented a language, but nobody knew what that language was saying. Then, a discovery in 1799 changed all of that. That was when a French solider unearthed what became known as the Rosetta Stone.

The Rosetta Stone was a remarkable find. It was a *stele*, a stone slab, on which was carved a single piece of text. The text was written over and over again in three different languages. This was the breakthrough that scientists needed. Knowing what the authors were trying to say and being able to compare known words with three ancient languages helped to break the code. It helped them understand what became known as the ancient hieroglyphic language. Here is how it works:

Imagine you have a document in a language you understand. Maybe it's a simple letter that starts with "*Dear Peter, please come home for dinner.*" Then, you find that same line in three different languages.

Spanish: Querido Peter, por favor vuelve a casa para la cena.

French: Cher Peter, s'il vous plaît revenir à la maison pour le dîner.

Italian: Caro Peter, ti aspettiamo a casa per cena.

By looking at all three languages and knowing what the original document was about, you can figure out that "cher" in French means "dear" in English.

The Rosetta Stone worked much in the same way.

Since then, the term "Rosetta Stone" has become an idiom in the English language. An idiom is an expression used to describe something in a culture. In this case, the term is used to describe the clue that is used to solve a mystery.

Answer the following questions about the story "Finding the Rosetta Stone." The weights show you how hard you will need to work to find each answer.

1. Based on what you learned from the passage, what is the Italian word for *dear*?

Ⓐ *claro*
Ⓑ *cher*
Ⓒ *caro*
Ⓓ *carus*

2. What is not an example of an idiom?

Ⓐ He is pulling my leg!
Ⓑ You should keep an eye out for the lost book.
Ⓒ You seem to have a chip on your shoulder.
Ⓓ This is a great book!

3. According to the passage, what is a *stele*?

Ⓐ a small sliver of rock
Ⓑ a slab of stone
Ⓒ a piece of pottery
Ⓓ a tomb

4. How many languages were found carved into the Rosetta Stone?

Ⓐ 3
Ⓑ 4
Ⓒ 2
Ⓓ 5

On the lines below, write your own question based on "Finding the Rosetta Stone." Circle the correct picture on the left to show the level of the question you wrote.

____

____

____

____

____

On a separate piece of paper . . .

- Write a sentence that includes the word *ancient.*
- Do you know more than one language? If so, what are the similarities between English and your other spoken language? If not, what other language would you most like to learn, and why?

History Passage #4

One Massive Mystery

A large circular structure sits in a field of grass deep in the English countryside. It is made of massive stones. These ancient rocks are nearly 5,000 years old, and some of the largest ones weigh as much 50 tons. Together, the stones form a monument called Stonehenge. It is one of the most famous sites in the world, attracting about a million visitors each year. It is also one of history's greatest mysteries.

How was Stonehenge built, and who built it? These are questions that still puzzle us to this day. With the knowledge we now have, we can determine that Stonehenge was built over a period of about 1,500 years. Construction began in about 3100 BCE and continued over various stages until about 1600 BCE. These were prehistoric times, so we don't have any written record of how or why the monument was built. Scientists have to piece together the evidence they can find in order to understand how Stonehenge came to be. The evidence, though, raises many questions that do not have simple answers:

- Why is the monument built from these particular stones? The huge stones that form Stonehenge do not come from the immediate area. They had to be moved over miles of rough terrain to get there.
- How were these massive stones moved such long distances? This was before modern equipment. The monument features several groups of three huge stones, two standing on end with another large stone placed across the top. How could this have been accomplished so long ago?
- What was the purpose of Stonehenge? There may be several answers to this question. It may have been used as a kind of observatory, for example. The monument seems to be aligned with the rising of the sun at certain times of the year. Stonehenge has likely also served as a sacred burial site at one time or another. A large number of bones and artifacts have been unearthed in the area.

Over the years, scientists and historians have continued to study Stonehenge in an attempt to learn more about its past. Will we ever fully solve the mystery of Stonehenge? For now, the answer to that question remains a mystery, too.

Answer the following questions about the story "One Massive Mystery." The weights show you how hard you will need to work to find each answer.

1. Based on the passage, what is the definition of *prehistoric*?

Ⓐ "mysterious"
Ⓑ "made of stone"
Ⓒ "before written records"
Ⓓ "very important"

2. If the year 3100 BCE was over 5,000 years ago, then how long ago was 1600 BCE?

Ⓐ about 3,600 years ago
Ⓑ about 2,000 years ago
Ⓒ about 1,600 years ago
Ⓓ about 1,000 years ago

3. Which question is not given in the passage as a reason why Stonehenge is mysterious?

Ⓐ Why were those rocks used?
Ⓑ How were the rocks moved?
Ⓒ Why was Stonehenge built?
Ⓓ Why do so many people visit Stonehenge?

4. An *analogy* is a comparison between two things. Look at the first part of this analogy to determine what the missing answer should be.

Stone is to *stones* as *mystery* is to ______________________.

Ⓐ *Stonehenge*
Ⓑ *puzzle*
Ⓒ *mysteries*
Ⓓ *mysterious*

On the lines below, write your own question based on "One Massive Mystery." Circle the correct picture on the left to show the level of the question you wrote.

____

____

____

____

____

On a separate piece of paper . . .

- Write a sentence that includes the word *massive.*
- Why do you think so many people visit Stonehenge each year? Write at least two sentences to explain your answer.

History Passage #5

The Story Behind the Beard

It has been about 150 years since U.S. president Abraham Lincoln died, but his face remains an iconic image. Most Americans can identify it immediately. So, what is it that makes Lincoln's face so memorable? Is it the narrow nose or the serious eyes? Is it the high forehead or the deep lines around his mouth? For many, it is the beard that distinguishes Abraham Lincoln's face from all others throughout history. Lincoln's mustache-less beard is such an iconic part of his image. It is hard to picture him without it. But until a few weeks before the presidential election of 1860, Abraham Lincoln did not have a beard. In fact, up until then, he had never grown one at any point in his life. So what (or who) changed Lincoln's mind and made him decide to grow facial hair? It was an 11-year-old girl he had not yet met.

Grace Bedell's father was a strong supporter of Abraham Lincoln. One day he brought home a picture of Lincoln and showed it to his 11-year-old daughter, Grace. She was immediately struck by the image of Lincoln's beardless face. She found it too thin and not very attractive. She said to her mother, "He would look better if he wore whiskers, and I mean to write and tell him so."

On October 15, 1860, Grace mailed a letter to Lincoln from her home in Westfield, New York. In it, she talked about her four brothers and her baby sister and how "if I was a man I would vote for you." She also asked him to grow a beard. She wrote, "All the ladies like whiskers and they would tease their husbands to vote for you and then you would be President." Abraham Lincoln received her letter, and on October 19, 1860, he wrote back. In his letter, he stated that he had never worn whiskers and he asked, "do you not think people would call it a silly affection if I were to begin it now?"

Despite Lincoln's question to Grace, he did begin to grow his whiskers. By the time he was sworn in as president in February of 1861, Lincoln had a full growth of beard along his jawline. It was at that time that Lincoln stopped in Grace's hometown with the hopes of seeing her. Several years later, Grace Bedell recalled what Abraham Lincoln said to her that day. "Gracie, " he said, "look at my whiskers. I have been growing them for you."

Answer the following questions about the story "The Story Behind the Beard." The weights show you how hard you will need to work to find each answer.

1. According to the passage, what does the word *iconic* mean?

Ⓐ facial
Ⓑ memorable
Ⓒ attractive
Ⓓ presidential

2. Where was Abraham Lincoln when he first met Grace Bedell in person?

Ⓐ the White House
Ⓑ Washington, D.C.
Ⓒ Westfield, New York
Ⓓ Gettysburg, Pennsylvania

3. In his letter to Grace, what seems to be Lincoln's thoughts about growing a beard?

Ⓐ He thinks it's a fantastic idea, and he'll start growing one immediately.
Ⓑ He's concerned that people will think he's trying to be someone he's not.
Ⓒ He's worried that a beard would look terrible on him, so he won't grow one.
Ⓓ He says he once had a beard, and he has been thinking about growing one again.

4. Which of these pieces of information can you infer from the story?

Ⓐ Everyone in Westfield voted for Abraham Lincoln in 1860.
Ⓑ Grace Bedell was not impressed by Lincoln's beard once she saw it.
Ⓒ Grace insisted that Lincoln visited her after he won the election.
Ⓓ Women could not vote in the presidential election of 1860.

On the lines below, write your own question based on "The Story Behind the Beard." Circle the correct picture on the left to show the level of the question you wrote.

____

____

____

____

____

On a separate piece of paper . . .

- Write a sentence that includes the word *memorable.*
- Picture a famous person who has an iconic look. You can choose someone from the past or someone who is alive and famous today. Name this person and tell what about his or her appearance is so iconic.

Biographical Passage #1

The Man Who Made Myths Cool

Rick Riordan was born on June 5, 1964, in San Antonio, Texas. Early on, he knew he wanted to write. He wrote his first short stories in middle school, and by high school, he was an editor for his school newspaper. When he went to college, he ended up majoring in both English and history. After college, he became a teacher. By teaching mythology, he shared the stories of gods and goddesses with kids for years. Eventually, however, he left the classroom and became one of the most famous fantasy authors of all time. His Percy Jackson books are one of the best-selling series in the world. They tell the story of a young boy who learns that he is the "half-blood" son to Poseidon, the god of ocean.

Rick was influenced early on by such books as *The Lord of the Rings* series, which he admits, he "probably read ten times!" He loved Greek and Roman mythology, and voraciously read fantasy and science fiction. He gobbled those stories up, reading everything he could get his hands on. His parents were also teachers, and they were artists, too. In other words, Rick Riordan came from a really creative family.

The stories we all have grown to love started out merely as bedtime tales for Riordan's kids. You see, he used to read Greek and Roman myths to his own children at night. When they ran out of traditional myths, his sons asked him to create his own. That is how Percy Jackson was born. Other areas of his life inspired him, too. When Rick was in college, he worked his summers as a music director at a summer camp. That camp would one day become the inspiration for another famous fictional camp. Camp Half-Blood was where the sons and daughters of gods and goddesses could leave their human parents for the summer to hang out with other demi-gods.

Rick Riordan says that he loves writing for kids, but he has not ruled out going back into the classroom as a teacher. "I love being a teacher," Rick has said in interviews. "But for now, the books are keeping me very busy."

Answer the following questions about the story "The Man Who Made Myths Cool." The weights show you how hard you will need to work to find each answer.

1. Based on the passage, what can you infer the phrase "has not ruled out" means?

Ⓐ disagrees with
Ⓑ thinks it could still happen
Ⓒ would never return to
Ⓓ has nice memories of

2. Based on the passage, what does the word *voraciously* mean?

Ⓐ slowly nibbled
Ⓑ sipped
Ⓒ ate quickly
Ⓓ cooked

3. Why are the campers called "half-bloods?"

Ⓐ They don't share the same interests.
Ⓑ They have both A and B blood types.
Ⓒ They only have ½ the amount of blood in their bodies as other kids.
Ⓓ One parent is human and the other is a Greek god or goddess.

4. Rick Riordan loved fantasy and science fiction. Based on what you know about those reading genres, what book title might have interested young Rick?

Ⓐ *The History of the Titanic*
Ⓑ *Gossiping Kids in Middle School*
Ⓒ *How to Succeed at Video Games*
Ⓓ *The Knight in the Night*

On the lines below, write your own question based on "The Man Who Made Myths Cool." Circle the correct picture on the left to show the level of the question you wrote.

____

____

____

____

____

On a separate piece of paper . . .

- Write a sentence that includes the word *mythology*.
- What are some places in your life that you could see becoming a setting for a story? Think of a location that would serve as a great location and create a bulleted list of sensory details that describe that place.

Biographical Passage #2

A Teacher for All Times

Aristotle was a famous philosopher who lived in ancient Greece. A *philosopher* is someone who studies the big questions about life and reality. They think hard about the world around them by focusing on abstract questions. In other words, they think about things that can't be touched. Here are some examples of abstract questions:

- What is truth?
- What is imagination?
- Can you think about nothing?
- If you had a different name, would you be a different person?
- Do we really have free will?
- Why does the universe exist?

Aristotle was born in about 384 BC. At 17 years old, he was sent to Athens to study. Athens was considered the academic center of the world, and that was where he soon became a student of Plato. Plato had been a student of Socrates. That is significant because Socrates was known to be one of the best teachers of all time. He passed on great knowledge to Plato, who in turn passed on great knowledge to Aristotle. When Aristotle became a teacher later on, the line of greatness continued.

As a teacher, Aristotle became an instructor to the Macedonian prince Alexander the Great. When Alexander the Great eventually conquered Athens, Aristotle was allowed to build his own school, the Lyceum in Athens. In the Lyceum, students studied everything from math to art, from philosophy to politics. The students wrote everything they learned down on scrolls. In this way, one of the greatest early libraries in the world was created. Aristotle wrote approximately 200 works, ranging in topics from ethics (thinking about right and wrong) to science.

Aristotle died in 322 BC, but we still study his philosophies even today. He may have taught only a handful of students during his lifetime, but his teachings continue on even centuries later.

Name: ________________________________ Biographical Passage #2

Answer the following questions about the story "A Teacher for All Times." The weights show you how hard you will need to work to find each answer.

1. Think about the line of great teachers. Who taught Aristotle's teacher?

Ⓐ Aristotle
Ⓑ Plato
Ⓒ Socrates
Ⓓ Athena

2. About how many years old was Aristotle when he died?

Ⓐ 26
Ⓑ 62
Ⓒ 59
Ⓓ 82

3. According to the passage, what is the meaning of an abstract topic?

Ⓐ a concept that you can't touch
Ⓑ an issue that you can't think about
Ⓒ a concept you can learn the answer to
Ⓓ an issue that is controversial

4. Which of these is an example of an abstract question?

Ⓐ How many apples are on that tree?
Ⓑ How do bees make honey?
Ⓒ How do I make a chocolate cake?
Ⓓ Is there such a thing as right and wrong?

On the lines below, write your own question based on "A Teacher for All Times." Circle the correct picture on the left to show the level of the question you wrote.

____

____

____

____

____

On a separate piece of paper . . .

- Write a sentence that includes the word *significant*.
- Look at any of the abstract philosophical questions in the passage. Select one and write your own response as a student of philosophy.

Biographical Passage #3

Her Words Live On

Since 1886, the Statue of Liberty has greeted visitors to the United States. This giant symbol of freedom towers atop an island in New York Harbor. In her right hand, Lady Liberty holds high a brightly lit torch. On her pedestal, or base, is inscribed a poem named "The New Colossus." This famous poem ends with these words:

. . . cries she
With silent lips. "Give me your tired, your poor,
Your huddled masses yearning to breathe free,
The wretched refuse of your teeming shore.
Send these, the homeless, tempest-tossed to me,
I lift my lamp beside the golden door!"

Written by a local poet named Emma Lazarus, "The New Colossus" is about taking people in and giving them a place to grow. It's about offering a place to "breathe free." For many immigrants who passed through New York Harbor on their way to a new life in the United States, Lazarus's words have rung true. Her words perfectly capture the hope that America represents.

Emma was born into a wealthy family in New York City on July 22, 1849. At a young age, Emma showed immense talent as a writer, and her parents encouraged her to pursue her work. At age 17, she published her first book of poetry. Four years later, Emma's second book became a big success. Throughout her 20s and 30s, she published many poems in books and magazines. She also became increasingly interested in helping those who did not grow up in a life of privilege like she had. This focus in her life led her to write "The New Colossus" in 1883. She donated the poem to help raise money to build the pedestal for the Statue of Liberty.

In 1887, while in Europe, Emma became very ill. She returned to the U.S., but she never got better. On November 19, 1887, Emma died. It was not until 1903 that "The New Colossus" was inscribed on the base of the Statue of Liberty.

Answer the following questions about the story "Her Words Live On." The weights show you how hard you will need to work to find each answer.

1. Based on information given in the passage, which of these statements is true?

Ⓐ Emma was alive when the statue was placed in New York Harbor.

Ⓑ Emma was alive when her poem was inscribed on the statue's base.

Ⓒ Emma Lazarus died while traveling in Europe.

Ⓓ The first book of poetry that Emma published was a big success.

2. Based on the passage, which word is the closest in meaning to *inscribed*?

Ⓐ greeted

Ⓑ donated

Ⓒ encouraged

Ⓓ written

3. How old was Emma Lazarus when she died?

Ⓐ 34

Ⓑ 37

Ⓒ 38

Ⓓ 54

4. In "The New Colossus," what symbol is used to represent the opportunity that life in the U.S. offers?

Ⓐ "silent lips"

Ⓑ "huddled masses"

Ⓒ "wretched refuse"

Ⓓ "golden door"

On the lines below, write your own question based on "Her Words Live On." Circle the correct picture on the left to show the level of the question you wrote.

____

____

____

____

____

On a separate piece of paper . . .

- Write a sentence that includes the word *immense*.
- Write about a building, statue, or landmark that you think is a great symbol of your country. Explain why you feel this way. (Choose something other than the Statue of Liberty.)

Biographical Passage #4

Bo Knows Greatness

Vincent "Bo" Jackson was born on November 30, 1962. As a young person, there were two ways in which Bo stood out from everyone else: his athletic ability and his stutter. Bo had trouble speaking smoothly, and this made him angry and frustrated. He felt that he didn't fit in. His athletic ability didn't help him blend in either. Bo could run faster, leap higher, throw harder, and hit a ball farther than anyone his age. He had so much talent in high school that the New York Yankees offered him a lot of money to play baseball for them. Instead, Bo chose to go to college. He attended Auburn University, where he excelled in football, baseball, and track. After college, Bo's professional career began.

From 1987–1990, Bo was a star at the highest level in two sports. As a football player for the Los Angeles Raiders of the NFL, he was one of the league's fastest, strongest running backs. It seemed as if he could run by anyone who chased him or run over anyone who got in his way. As a baseball player for the Kansas City Royals, he was a powerful home-run hitter who made spectacular leaping catches in the outfield. Bo was such a unique athlete that he is still the only person to be both an All-Star in Major League Baseball and an All-Pro in the NFL. Bo also gained fame for his role in several TV commercials for Nike, a shoe company. The commercials were based on the idea that Bo "knows" how to be great at just about everything.

Bo's greatness as an athlete came to a stunning end on January 13, 1991. During an important football game, he was tackled and dragged down after a 34-yard run. His left hip came out of its socket and then popped back in. A blood vessel was severed. This terrible injury damaged his hip permanently. Bo's football career was over.

Bo went through a tough, grueling process in an effort to continue his baseball career. He was able to play again, this time for the Chicago White Sox. But his once-great speed was gone. Bo retired from baseball in 1994.

Of all his accomplishments, Bo has said that he is most proud of what he has done off the field. Unlike many star athletes, Bo has never been in trouble with the law. He and his wife raised four children. He became a successful businessman. He overcame his stuttering problem and gave a speech in front of thousands at Auburn in 2009. Despite losing his athletic gifts to injury, Bo worked hard to become great at other things in life.

Answer the following questions about the story "Bo Knows Greatness." The weights show you how hard you will need to work to find each answer.

1. For which team did Bo first become a star player in Major League Baseball?

Ⓐ New York Yankees
Ⓑ Kansas City Royals
Ⓒ Chicago White Sox
Ⓓ Los Angeles Raiders

2. The passage says that Bo's greatness came to a "stunning end." This means that his greatness as an athlete

Ⓐ shocked sports fans.
Ⓑ became less over the years.
Ⓒ ended when he retired from baseball.
Ⓓ ended suddenly and in a shocking way.

3. How old was Bo when he suffered the hip injury that ended his football career? (Hint: Pay close attention to the month he was born in.)

Ⓐ 25 years old
Ⓑ 28 years old
Ⓒ 29 years old
Ⓓ 32 years old

4. The passage uses the word *grueling*. Which of these words is most like *grueling*?

Ⓐ hungry
Ⓑ smooth
Ⓒ difficult
Ⓓ powerful

On the lines below, write your own question based on "Bo Knows Greatness." Circle the correct picture on the left to show the level of the question you wrote.

____

____

____

____

____

On a separate piece of paper . . .

- Write a sentence that includes the word *unique*.
- Who is the greatest athlete you have ever seen? Is it someone you have seen in person or only on TV? Is it someone the world knows about? Give reasons for your choice.

Informational Passage #1

What Is Microlending?

Donating to charity used to just mean giving away a little bit of money to an organization that is doing something good for the world. However, a new, 21st-century way to help others is gaining in popularity. It's called *microlending*, and it is a growing trend online. It is a way to assist others as they start up their own businesses. Websites help donors find people who need investors. An investor is someone who gives money to help someone pay to develop an idea. Here is how it works:

1. A person wants to donate a little money, but doesn't know who needs it.
2. A microlending site provides lists of people looking for donors.
3. A person can read about folks looking for help in starting their business. They can search by location, kind of business, gender, etc.
4. The donor sends money to the microlending site. The site then gives it to the person far away to help them.
5. The person, with the help of many donations from people like you, starts their business and begins to pay back their loan.
6. The donor gets their money back!

Now, that donor has the choice to either lend that money to someone else or keep it! Either way, he or she knows that the loan helped someone become a business owner.

In other words, if a person, even a child with the help of an adult*, has $25 to loan, he or she can go to a website and begin searching for someone to help. You might help a farmer in Africa buy grain to expand his or her crops. You might help a woman in Asia start a clothing business. You might aid someone in starting a unique school for struggling children. With these new microlending sites, you can reach across miles to lend a helping hand to a person with big dreams.

**Remember, if you ever think about visiting a microlending site, make sure you have an adult with you. Any website that deals with money is one that needs adult supervision.*

Answer the following questions about the story "What Is Microlending?" The weights show you how hard you will need to work to find each answer.

1. Based on the passage, what does *investor* mean?

Ⓐ someone who asks for money to start a business
Ⓑ someone who loans money to others to help a business grow
Ⓒ someone who farms in Africa
Ⓓ a website that works to connect people from all over the world

2. Why is there an asterisk (*) in the final paragraph of the passage?

Ⓐ to encourage the reader to search online
Ⓑ to help the reader understand how microlending works
Ⓒ to draw the reader's attention to the bottom of the passage where there is important information to read
Ⓓ to tell the reader that this is the passage's most important sentence

3. Based on the passage, what does "growing trend" mean?

Ⓐ more and more people are doing it
Ⓑ it's getting smaller in popularity
Ⓒ it's hard to find
Ⓓ the company is getting bigger

4. What is not listed as a way to search on a site for someone to invest in?

Ⓐ gender
Ⓑ location
Ⓒ kind of business
Ⓓ favorite website

On the lines below, write your own question based on "What Is Microlending?" Circle the correct picture on the left to show the level of the question you wrote.

____

____

____

____

____

On a separate piece of paper . . .

- Write a sentence that includes the word *loan.*
- Have you ever helped others in need, either by performing a community service or by making a donation? Write about how you found the person you helped and what you did to help that person.

Informational Passage #2

Mastering an Ancient Art

Would you consider your handwriting to be a form of art? You probably wouldn't, but there is a type of writing that is thought of this way. It is called *calligraphy*, and it is used all over the world. It is especially popular in such Asian countries as China, Japan, and Korea. In order to master calligraphy, one must combine the creativity of an artist with the technical skill of a craftsman. Each character must be written beautifully and with great precision.

The use of calligraphy in China dates back thousands of years. At times, it has even been considered the highest and purest form of painting. In fact, original writings by famous Chinese calligraphers can be worth a lot of money and are often hung on walls, just like paintings.

As with any art or skill, there are tools that one needs to use. Calligraphers use four basic tools. Together, they are known as the Four Treasures of the Study:

- **Paper** – A special paper called *xuanzhi* is preferred. It can be made from materials like elm, rice, and bamboo.
- **Ink** – Calligraphy ink is traditionally black, and it comes in sticks. The sticks must be rubbed with water until the right consistency is produced.
- **Ink Stone** – An ink stick is rubbed against this stone or ceramic piece until a liquid form is produced.
- **Brush** – The brush is used to apply the ink to the paper. The hairs of the brush come from such animals as rabbits, deer, tigers, or ducks. The handle can be made of bamboo, ivory, silver, or gold.

These tools, along with years of practice, are necessary in order for the mastery of this art form. One of the best ways to practice is by writing the Chinese character *yong*. This character stands for the word "forever" or "eternity." In order to write this character, one must use the eight most basic strokes needed by calligraphers. These strokes have such names as "Iron Pillar" and "The Tiger's Tooth" and "Bird Pecking."

Answer the following questions about the story "Mastering an Ancient Art." The weights show you how hard you will need to work to find each answer.

1. Based on the way it is used in the passage, what does the word *character* mean?

Ⓐ "a printed letter or symbol"
Ⓑ "a person in a book, play, or movie"
Ⓒ "a person's good reputation"
Ⓓ "an interesting or amusing person"

2. What are the Four Treasures of the Study?

Ⓐ bamboo, ivory, silver, gold
Ⓑ rabbit, deer, tiger, duck
Ⓒ ink, ink stone, paper, pencil
Ⓓ paper, brush, ink, ink stone

3. Which of these is not named as one of the eight basic strokes of calligraphy?

Ⓐ "The Tiger's Tooth"
Ⓑ "Sleeping Dog"
Ⓒ "Iron Pillar"
Ⓓ "Bird Pecking"

4. Which of these words has the opposite meaning of the Chinese character *yong*?

Ⓐ forever
Ⓑ permanent
Ⓒ eternity
Ⓓ ending

On the lines below, write your own question based on "Mastering an Ancient Art." Circle the correct picture on the left to show the level of the question you wrote.

____

____

____

____

____

On a separate piece of paper . . .

- Write a sentence that includes the word *mastery*.
- Write your name in the most artistic and interesting way you can.

Informational Passage #3

From Postcards to Pizza

Most of us have bought something from a vending machine at some point. These handy machines offer quick and easy snacks and beverages for a relatively low price. But while we may think of chips and candy and soda when we hear the words "vending machine," these contraptions have always dispensed more than just food.

So how did vending machines begin? The modern vending machine really was first put into use in London, England, in the early 1880s. That first machine sold postcards. The first machine put into use in the United States began selling packs of gum in 1888 in New York City. From there, vending machines took off. Here are some of the major innovations and milestones that vending machines achieved during the 20th century:

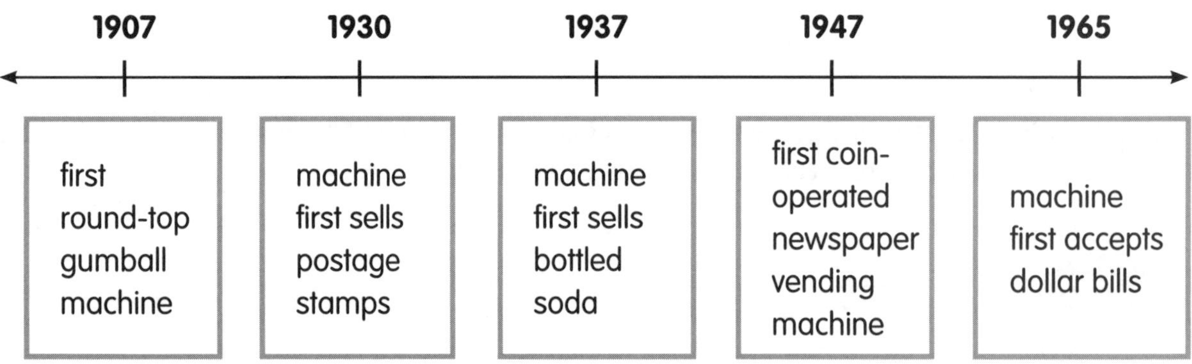

Today's vending machines can give out everything from mobile phones to bicycles. And the food that these machines give out is not simply chips and candy and soda. Some dispense meat, raw eggs, or freshly baked pizza. There is even a vending machine in Maine where customers can use a claw to pick out a live lobster.

Where will vending machines go from here? The future is most likely bright for these contraptions. They are convenient to use and cheap to operate. Vending-machine owners do not have to pay employees to work them. They can be open 24 hours a day, 7 days a week.

Answer the following questions about the story "From Postcards to Pizza." The weights show you how hard you will need to work to find each answer.

1. Based on the passage, you can infer that a synonym for *vending* would be

Ⓐ buying.
Ⓑ selling.
Ⓒ operating.
Ⓓ using.

2. Which is *not* given as a reason why vending machines may have a bright future?

Ⓐ They are always open.
Ⓑ They are cheap to operate.
Ⓒ People find them convenient to use.
Ⓓ People would rather buy from a machine than a person.

3. The passage states that vending machines "took off" in the 20th century. What does this phrase suggest about vending machines?

Ⓐ They were used a lot more.
Ⓑ They flew up into the air.
Ⓒ They removed something.
Ⓓ They stayed home from work.

4. According to the timeline, what could vending machines *not* do before 1950?

Ⓐ give you change for a dollar bill
Ⓑ sell you a newspaper
Ⓒ sell you a bottled soda
Ⓓ dispense gumballs

On the lines below, write your own question based on "From Postcards to Pizza." Circle the correct picture on the left to show the level of the question you wrote.

____

____

____

____

____

On a separate piece of paper . . .

- Write a sentence that includes the word *contraption.*
- If you could design a vending machine that sold some of your favorite things, what would it sell? Draw a picture of your ideal vending machine.

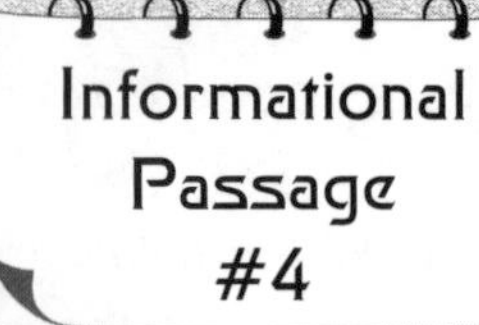

A Dangerous Delicacy

Would you ever knowingly eat something that could make you sick or even kill you? For most people, their immediate answer would be "Of course not!" For others, there is one fish that is worth the risk, and it is called *fugu*.

Fugu is the Japanese name for the blowfish. Some parts of the blowfish are so poisonous that they can kill anyone who eats them. The blowfish's liver, for example, is particularly dangerous. As a result, it has been illegal since 1984 to serve the fugu's liver in a restaurant in Japan. Yet, the liver is considered by many to be a delicacy. This means that people think it is a special treat. They are willing to pay lots of money and risk their lives to taste it.

Chefs who safely prepare fugu in restaurants must possess great skill and special equipment. A fugu chef uses a knife with a long, very thin blade to slice the safe parts of the fish away from the unsafe parts. The poisoned parts must not touch the safe parts, or else they will contaminate them. They will transfer the poison onto those parts and make them unsafe to touch or eat.

As a result, being a fugu chef in Japan can be a dangerous occupation. It is also a very high honor. In order to even be allowed to do this job, a chef must complete a rigorous training process. He or she must spend three years learning how to slice the fish correctly and demonstrating this knowledge by taking tests. Fewer than half are able to pass the tests. And then, at the end of training, the chefs take the ultimate exam: they must prepare a plate of fugu and eat it. Some chefs die while taking this test!

So what does a dish of this dangerous delicacy look and taste like? Fugu is usually served raw. (Cooking it would not destroy the poison anyway.) It is usually sliced so thin and so delicately that the pieces are nearly transparent. You can almost see right through them. These extremely thin pieces are then arranged in artistic patterns on attractive plates. As for the taste, some people consider fugu to be supremely delicious. Others are not impressed. The Emperor of Japan might not know; it is the one food that by law he is not allowed to eat.

Answer the following questions about the story "A Dangerous Delicacy." The weights show you how hard you will need to work to find each answer.

1. What is the final test a fugu chef must take in order to complete his or her training?

Ⓐ serving fugu to the Emperor of Japan
Ⓑ serving a dish of fugu liver to the teacher
Ⓒ eating fugu he or she has prepared
Ⓓ sharpening a fugu knife correctly

2. Which of the following could be described as *rigorous*?

Ⓐ using a fugu knife correctly
Ⓑ eating fugu liver without getting sick
Ⓒ eating a delicacy
Ⓓ training to be a fugu chef in Japan

3. Which of the following is *not* a way to ensure that a piece of blowfish is safe to eat?

Ⓐ cooking it for a long time
Ⓑ slicing it correctly
Ⓒ having a trained chef prepare it
Ⓓ keeping it away from poisonous parts

4. Based on how the word is used in the story, which of the following things could be called *transparent*?

Ⓐ a metal knife
Ⓑ a paper cup
Ⓒ a glass dish
Ⓓ a wooden bowl

On the lines below, write your own question based on "A Dangerous Delicacy." Circle the correct picture on the left to show the level of the question you wrote.

____

____

____

____

____

On a separate piece of paper . . .

- Write a sentence that includes the word *delicacy*.
- Do you think it is a reasonable law that says the Emperor of Japan cannot eat fugu? Give reasons for your answer.

Answer Key

Accept appropriate responses for the final three entries on the question-and-answer pages.

A Storytelling Tradition (page 11)
1. C **3.** B
2. C **4.** D

Pluto: Planet or Not? (page 13)
1. B **3.** C
2. B **4.** C

My Foot Fell Asleep! (page 15)
1. C **3.** D
2. A **4.** A

More Than a Long Neck (page 17)
1. D **3.** B
2. C **4.** A

Light Before Sound (page 19)
1. B **3.** D
2. B **4.** D

How to Debug a Computer (page 21)
1. A **3.** C
2. C **4.** D

A Female Pharaoh? (page 23)
1. C **3.** A
2. D **4.** C

The Library of Alexandria (page 25)
1. D **3.** D
2. A **4.** B

Finding the Rosetta Stone (page 27)
1. C **3.** B
2. D **4.** A

One Massive Mystery (page 29)
1. C **3.** D
2. A **4.** C

The Story Behind the Beard (page 31)
1. B **3.** B
2. C **4.** D

The Man Who Made Myths Cool (page 33)
1. B **3.** D
2. C **4.** D

A Teacher for All Times (page 35)
1. C **3.** A
2. B **4.** D

Her Words Live On (page 37)
1. A **3.** C
2. D **4.** D

Bo Knows Greatness (page 39)
1. B **3.** B
2. D **4.** C

What Is Microlending? (page 41)
1. B **3.** A
2. C **4.** D

Mastering an Ancient Art (page 43)
1. A **3.** B
2. D **4.** D

From Postcards to Pizza (page 45)
1. B **3.** A
2. D **4.** A

A Dangerous Delicacy (page 47)
1. C **3.** A
2. D **4.** C